TEACH YOURSELF
Bluegrass Fiddle

by Matt Glaser

Teach yourself authentic bluegrass. Clear instructions from a professional; basics,
right- and left-hand techniques, solos, backup, personal advice on performance, and much more.
Plus a complete selection of the best bluegrass songs and tunes to learn from.

PLAYBACK+
Speed • Pitch • Balance • Loop

To access audio visit:
www.halleonard.com/mylibrary

Enter Code
7457-3841-0386-7744

TEACH YOURSELF
Bluegrass Fiddle

by Matt Glaser

Teach yourself authentic bluegrass. Clear instructions from a professional; basics,
right- and left-hand techniques, solos, backup, personal advice on performance, and much more.
Plus a complete selection of the best bluegrass songs and tunes to learn from.

Photography by Randall Wallace and Herb Wise
Project editors: Peter Pickow and Ed Lozano
Musical contractor: Bob Grant
Interior Design and layout: Don Giller

ISBN 978-0-8256-0324-2

Visit Hal Leonard Online at
www.halleonard.com

Contact us:
Hal Leonard
7777 West Bluemound Road
Milwaukee, WI 53213
Email: info@halleonard.com

In Europe, contact:
Hal Leonard Europe Limited
42 Wigmore Street
Marylebone, London, W1U 2RN
Email: info@halleonardeurope.com

In Australia, contact:
Hal Leonard Australia Pty. Ltd.
4 Lentara Court
Cheltenham, Victoria, 3192 Australia
Email: info@halleonard.com.au

Audio Track Listing

Audio Personnel

Antoine Silverman: Fiddle
Bob Grant: Mandolin, Guitar, and Vocals
Tony Trischka: Banjo
Matt Weiner: Bass

Table of Contents

Introduction

This book is intended for those people who have had some experience playing the violin and would now like to play bluegrass fiddle. This category might include people with violin training gained in school, old-timey fiddle players, or even experienced classical violinists. If you are familiar with the basics of the instrument, then this volume can serve as a source book of tunes and songs that are part of the bluegrass repertoire. In addition, it provided you with breaks for every tune, so that you can see how to structure a solo and begin to improvise on your own.

To avoid the use of sixteenth notes, which many beginners find confusing, the majority of tunes have been written out in 4/4, or common time. When you are first learning the tunes, tap your foot on every beat; when you feel more comfortable with the music you can increase the tempo and tap your foot on every other beat.

Musical Notation

This book makes use of standard musical notation; if you're comfortable reading music, skip this part. If you don't know how to read, or feel rusty at it, here's a brief refresher course.

Music is expressed by means of symbols called notes. These notes are placed on a staff of five lines and four spaces; in this book we will only use the treble, or G clef, so called because it encircles the second line from the bottom and establishes the note G.

G Clef

The rest of the notes on the staff are:

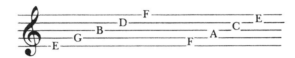

Particularly astute readers will notice that the letters for the spaces, when read from bottom to top, spell FACE. (Those readers should also notice that the letters for the lines don't spell anything at all, unless, of course, you're Welsh.) Some crafty music teacher from eons ago devised a sentence to help the beginner remember the notes on the lines of the treble clef; that deathless prose is: "Every Good Boy Does Fine." To extend the limits of the treble clef, leger lines are added above or below it.

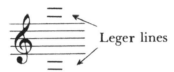

Leger lines

The duration, or time value, of a note is indicated by its shape. A whole note is sounded twice as long as a half note; a half note is sounded twice as long as a quarter note, etc. Rests are intervals of silence during which you do not play. Each note and its corresponding rest are equal in duration.

Types of notes and rests:

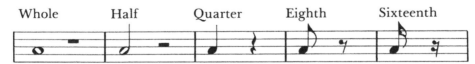

A dot placed after and alongside a note increases its time value by one half.

A dotted half note equals three quarter notes.

Whenever the pitch of a note is to be varied by a half step, the change is indicated by placing before the note one of the following accidentals:

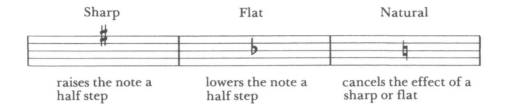

Sharp	Flat	Natural
raises the note a half step	lowers the note a half step	cancels the effect of a sharp or flat

A tie is a curved line joining two notes of the same pitch that are to be sounded continuously for the total value of both notes.

Ties are not to be confused with slurs, which are bow markings indicating that the notes slurred are to be played on one bow-stroke. Down-bows and up-bows are indicated by the traditional markings:

down bow   up bow

The only odd musical notation device used in this book is the indication for a slide. Every time you see a little arrow pointing up to a note from below, it means that you should slide into the note from slightly below the written pitch. If you listen to bluegrass fiddling for any amount of time, your ear will tell you how much to slide.

Some Words About Reading Music

All music is meant to be played and heard, and the best way to learn any music is by listening and imitating. This is especially true in bluegrass where this is no tradition of writing out compositions, but rather passing them on from musician to musician by ear.

Just as a piece of correspondence in itself cannot convey the inflection, intonation or shades of meaning in the writer's voice, so written music is lacking when used alone. The breaks and tunes presented in this book will be useful only when they are used in conjunction with lost of listening. Recordings are one way (a bunch of good ones are listed in the back); and inundating yourself with the sound and feel of fiddling—with their help—is of primary importance. Playing with other people is also a necessity. Bluegrass is a form of chamber music, where five people play together to form a "band" sound, each instrument serving a different function in the overall scheme. So, treat the music written here as a signpost to a certain sound, by no means rigid and inflexible. Try to add something of your own to every break you take, because in this music there is unlimited room for musical individuality; and most of all, have a good time with it!

Short History of Bluegrass Fiddle

Bill Monroe, of Rosine, Kentucky, is the man almost single-handedly responsible for the birth of bluegrass He combined elements of mountain, black, Irish and other musics to form a high-powered sound that people soon began to call bluegrass, after the name of Bill's band, the Bluegrass Boys.

One of Bill's uncles, Pen Vendever, played the fiddle and had a major influence on Bill's musical growth; largely as a result of Pen's inspiration, Monroe has made the fiddle a predominant sound in his music.

The first person who can safely be called a bluegrass fiddler is Chubby Wise. Chubby came to Monroe's band with a sweet singing tone, great technique and a background as a swing fiddler. With Monroe's help, he developed the bluesy sound that is the basis for modern bluegrass fiddling. Soon, other fiddlers turned up who were playing distinctly bluegrass fiddle, as opposed to old-timey or country style. Admittedly, some of them, such as Charlie Cline, "Red" Taylor, Gordon Terry and others, were firmly rooted in mountain fiddling and maintained some of that rawness in their bluegrass playing. Others strove for a more polished sound and more sophisticated use of the fiddle's capabilities; Dale Potter, Benny Martin, Kenny Baker and Bobby Hicks are some of these fiddlers.

The 1950s were really the Grand Old Days for bluegrass music and consequently for bluegrass fiddling. Some great fiddlers active during this period (in addition to those already mentioned) were Paul Warren, Tater Tate, "Mac" Magaha, Jim Buchanan and Scotty Stoneman. The '50s also saw the introduction of twin and triple fiddling into bluegrass. Multiple fiddles had been used in Western Swing prior to this time, but the sound of multiple fiddles in bluegrass was very different; less sweet and more bluesy and lonesome. The first Bill Monroe record session to make use of triple fiddles was in 1954; the vocal numbers were *Close By* and *My Little Georgia Rose.* The first bluegrass instrumentals recorded with triple fiddles were *Tall Timber* and *Brown Country Breakdown,* with the fine fiddling being done by Vassar Clements, Bobby Hicks and Gordon Terry.

The playing of jazz violinists Stephane Grappelli and Joe Venuti has always had a big influence on bluegrass fiddlers, from Chubby Wise through Kenny Baker up to some of the young fiddlers like Ricky Skaggs. When Chubby Wise plays a lick like this one, it becomes immediately evident that he's absorbed much of the feel of Venuti's playing.

Kenny Baker has often said that as a young man he studied and admired the playing of Stephane Grappelli; a Baker lick like this one points to that influence.

Vassar Clements, Dale Potter and Richard Greene are among other fiddlers who have been influenced by swing fiddling and swing music in general.

Today's young bluegrass fiddlers are even more musically aware than their older counterparts. It's not uncommon to find a young fiddler who listens to jazz and classical music in addition to bluegrass. These fiddlers have their ears open in much the same way that early bluegrass fiddlers did, drawing upon the varied musical styles that surround them.

Beginning Bluegrass Fiddle

If you are just beginning to play bluegrass fiddle, it's important to have in your mind a clear idea of what separates bluegrass from other kinds of music. The instrumentation of a standard bluegrass band consists of banjo, guitar, mandolin, bass and fiddle; all the instruments, to varying degrees, play solos and backup. Bluegrass can be distinguished from old-timey music in a number of ways. Old-timey bands generally have a loose-as-a-goose sound with most of the instruments playing the melody all the time. Bluegrass, on the other hand, is a rhythmically tight quintet sound with a vocal center where each instrument has a distinct role. The fiddle often serves to complement and imitate the vocal line. Like the human voice, the fiddle can naturally sustain a tone or produce a tone in other than a percussive manner. (This is something that none of the other bluegrass instruments can do.)

Bluegrass fiddling has a number of qualities that distinguish it from other kinds of fiddling; the foremost of these is its bluesy sound. The element of blues was pretty much absent from traditional fiddling until the arrival of "Fiddlin" Arthur Smith, who inspired the early bluegrassers, like Chubby Wise. Listening to modern fiddlers such as Vassar Clements, Richard Greene or Tex Logan should help in understanding the role blues plays in fiddling.

A higher level of technical ability is needed in bluegrass than in any other kind of country fiddling. A great deal of bluegrass is played in keys like B♭, B and C, keys that are very challenging on the fiddle. In addition, much of this music goes very fast and demands a sustained drive that takes a lot of stamina. This virtuosic kind of fiddling has some precedent in the playing of old-timers like Clark Kessinger, but it wasn't until bluegrassers such as Scotty Stoneman that super-high speeds became commonplace.

One element in bluegrass that attracts a lot of people is improvisation. Where in old-timey music (as in classical music) the performer is basically an interpreter of some precomposed melody, in bluegrass he or she has the opportunity to improvise most of what he or she plays. Bluegrass more closely resembles jazz in this respect; both musics emphasize chord-oriented improvisation.

However, bluegrass is an extremely stylized form of music and the improvisation that goes on always remains within a certain framework. There are stock licks that every bluegrass fiddler uses to construct a break, and these licks can be traced to specific people. In my mind, Chubby Wise and Benny Martin are the fiddlers most responsible for the sound and feel of bluegrass fiddling.

Hopefully, the breaks and tunes in this book will help you realize a little bit of bluegrass flavor in your playing; however, since written music poorly conveys certain subtleties of bluegrass fiddling, I'd like to discuss some common technical problems and their solutions.

Most people approaching bluegrass fiddling have had some experience playing the instrument, either classical training or old-timey playing. There are some basic techniques in bluegrass that people from both backgrounds should learn.

The Use of the Bow

In any kind of violin or fiddle playing, the majority of technical problems that one encounters lies in the use of the bow. Tone production and phrasing, two crucial elements in any kind of music, are controlled totally by the bow.

Most good bluegrass fiddlers hold their bows in something similar to the classical manner (see photo).

Some players keep the thumb under the frog; others have it touching the stick. The old-timey fiddler who holds his or her bow way up the stick is well-advised to move his or her hand down near the frog. This is important because it permits the use of the entire stick and allows you to play kick-offs, right at the frog, where you have the most control and can get the most biting attack. The use of the whole bow is also crucial in slow or medium tempo songs, where a singing melodic line is called for.

Bluegrass fiddling generally requires a richer and sweeter tone than old-timey, and one exercise that can be very helpful in this direction is just to draw the bow from the frog to the tip and back again, listening for purity of tone and minimal bow noise. As you draw the bow, watch to see that it remains pretty much parallel to the bridge throughout its entire length.

There are three factors that control tone production on the violin: (1) the speed of the bow stroke, (2) the pressure of the bow on the strings, and (3) the point at which the bow contacts the strings. If you experiment with these factors and vary them to suit your ear, you'll gain control over a wide range of different tone colors. Most good bluegrass fiddlers use less bow speed and more bow pressure than either old-timey or classical players; they also (in general) play close to the bridge. These factors help produce the rich, intense sound that the music demands.

Phrasing with the Bow

Since bluegrass is such a highly expressive and improvisatory type of music, one's bowing should be flexible enough to accommodate many different types of phrases. The most basic kind of phrasing used in bluegrass involves playing the melody of a song in a vocal manner, with some degree of ornamentation. Peter Rowan (who played guitar and sang lead with Bill Monroe in the '60s) said some interesting things about the relationship of singing and fiddle playing in an interview with Pete Wernick of *Country Cookin'*: "To me, bluegrass singing is like fiddle playing. It's like a few short words and a long held out thing, you know, like 'It was in the spr*iiiii*ng, one sunny d*aaaaa*y'—a short bust of a few notes and then a long held-out thing, 'Sweetheart of m*iiii*ne . . . .' When Bill [Monroe[teaches fiddle parts and stuff, he sings them, he teaches the fiddle part from sort of like a singing orientation. It's like these short little scales, up to a certain note, the note held and the next melody line coming in after that."

Another kind of phrasing that occurs often in bluegrass is the kind used in playing a driving fiddle tune, or instrumental. Both old-timey fiddlers and classical violinists often have difficulty in getting that element of drive in their playing, and I think the problem lies in their use of symmetrical, or predetermined bowings. Where an old-timey fiddler might play an eighth note passage bowed like this:

or a classical violinist like this:

The bluegrass fiddler would probably play it as here, with the number of notes slurred changing constantly:

To familiarize yourself with this approach, I would suggest taking a fiddle tune and varying the bowing in as many ways as you can. For example, try the first few bars of *June Apple* with a straight shuffle bowing (two notes slurred, two notes separate):

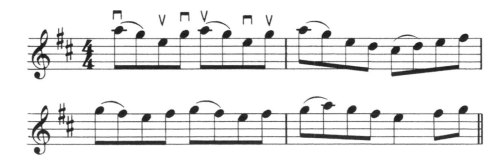

Now try it three notes slurred, three separate:

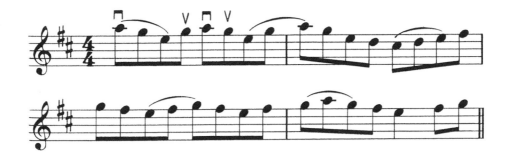

Finally, try it with a combination of different bowings:

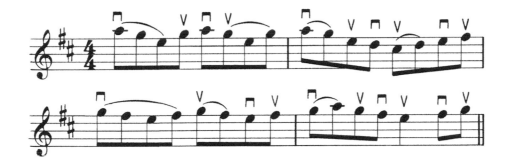

It's a good idea, in any driving tune, to keep pressure on the bow at the moment of bow change as this will sustain the sound.

The Left Hand

Probably the most important left-hand technique in bluegrass fiddling is the slide. Sliding into certain notes helps create the bluesy sound so desirable in this music; some players, like Vassar Clements and Scotty Stoneman, slide so often that it becomes the major identifying factor in their sound. Blues are an important element in bluegrass, but since they're completely absent from classical music, the violinist often has difficulty getting used to sliding as an expressive device. The best remedy for this is just to listen to the playing of the great bluesy fiddlers until that sound seems natural to you.

It seems that the interval into which fiddlers most often slide is the third of the chord (C♯ in the key of A, D♯ in B, etc.). The third is the interval that controls whether a chord is major or minor, and sliding creates an ambiguity that our ears identify as bluesy. As an example of this, play the passage below as written, without slides:

Now try the same passage, sliding into the third from a half-step below:

You can see that the slide gives this passage a bluegrassy flavor that was absent previously.

Intonation in Difficult Keys

As mentioned earlier, a great deal of bluegrass is played in the keys of B♭, B and C, where singers can get that high, lonesome sound. Playing in these keys often presents intonation problems for the old-timey fiddler who's accustomed to playing in open string keys like G, D, and A.

It's very helpful, especially in these keys, to establish a feeling of "frame" in your left hand. Let's say you're in the key of B. Place your first finger on the note B on the A string; then, without moving your hand, place your pinky on the B note on the E string. You have one octave of a B major scale right at your fingertips.

When playing out of this position, keep your fingers curved and fingertips close to the fingerboard, avoiding any undue strain on the pinky. For the sake of your intonation, be extremely cognizant of the distance between half steps and whole steps in these keys. The fingering for an A major scale is:

Notice that there is a whole step between the second and third fingers and a half step between the third and fourth fingers in the B major scale below.

Double Stops

Playing two notes on the fiddle simultaneously is called double-stopping. Benny Martin, who played with Flatt and Scruggs, was the first fiddler in bluegrass to fully exploit the use of double stops; he stresses the need to "get an open sound and let the fiddle ring." Fiddlers use the natural resonance of the instrument by playing double stops and octaves using one open string, and especially by playing stopped notes in unison with the open strings:

(That $^0_4$ fingering will occur many times throughout the music in this book.)

If you find that you're having difficulty playing a certain double stop in tune, play one note of the two alone. Check the pitch with one of the open strings and, when you're sure that first note is in tune, add the other note. (It's easy to make the mistake of frantically adjusting a double stop without even isolating the note that's out of tune.)

When playing double stops, avoid cramping or tensing your hand; no amount of pressing or gripping will get the notes in tune. If you relax your hand, you'll be able to make whatever adjustments are needed to achieve good intonation.

Vibrato

Vibrato is the rapid back and forth movement of the finger, hand or arm that starts at a particular pitch, lowers the pitch slightly, and then returns to the original pitch. (The vibrato should never go above the pitch being played as this would give the music a slightly seasick quality.)

Vibrato isn't used nearly as much in bluegrass as in classical music, so the violinist coming to fiddling often has to cut down on his use of it. In bluegrass, vibrato is used to give a richer, fuller sound to a melodic line in a slow or medium tempo tune; it can be dispensed with altogether in fast tunes.

For the old-timey fiddler who is completely unfamiliar with this technique, the main thing to strive for is a relaxed and natural vibrato, not one that is forced or tense. One exercise to help you achieve this is to gently and slowly oscillate your hand back and forth. (This should feel good, as if you were giving your hand a massage.) When you feel comfortable doing this slowly, then gradually increase the speed (but not the tension) of your vibrato.

Philadelphia Folk Festival

Fiddle Tunes

I've included a good number of fiddle tunes (fourteen, to be exact) in this book, because these tunes are an important part of any bluegrass fiddler's repertoire. These tunes have proven to be incredibly durable; for example, *Soldier's Joy* can be traced back to the year 1779 in the British Isles, where it was called *The King's Head*. In addition to their function as music for dancing, modern day fiddlers have added new meaning to these tunes by using them as themes for complex sets of variations.

This is exemplified by such Texas fiddlers as Uncle Eck Robertson, who, with his 1922 version of *Sally Goodin*, became the first country musician ever to record. Robertson used to introduce the tune with a little anecdote:

"Seems that Sally was being courted by two men, both fiddlers. Well, she couldn't make up her mind so she told them to start fiddling and she would marry the winner. That old boy named Goodin won, and true to her word, she married him. Since then, there have been thirteen generations of Goodins and so I'm going to play *Sally Goodin* thirteen different ways."

It's common practice among today's Texas fiddlers to play *Sally Goodin* with at least thirteen distinct variations. Those variations are all on two basic parts, however, and those two parts are what I've included here. most fiddle tunes are composed of two parts, each eight measures long, with both sections played twice through; this means that a standard fiddle tune, played once, is 32 bars long and has an AABB structure. All the tunes in the next section conform to this structure, except for *Fire on the Mountain,* which has a two-bar tag at the end of the second phrase.

The breaks to these tunes contain techniques that progress from simple single line (*Soldier's Joy*), easy double stops (*Cripple Creek*), and simple variations (*Turkey in the Straw*), to complex variation (*Bill Cheatem, Arkansas Traveller, Salt River*) and complex double stops (*Sally Goodin*). As with most of the tunes in this book, I've left the bowing to the discretion of each player, but I will suggest that fiddle tunes can generally be played with a standard shuffle bowing: two notes slurred, two notes separate.

Enjoy!

Soldier's Joy

Key of D
Melody

Break

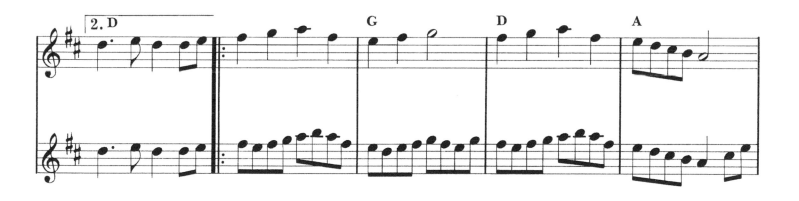

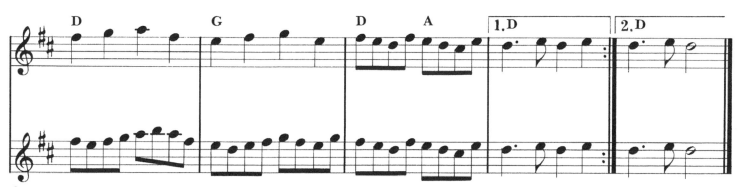

Old Joe Clark

Key of A
Melody

© Amsco Music Publishing Company, 1978

Cripple Creek

Key of A
Melody

Break

Fire on the Mountain

Key of A
Melody

Break

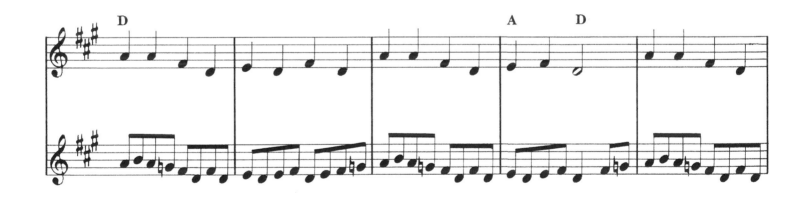

Turkey in the Straw

Key of G

Blackberry Blossom

Arkansas Traveller

Key of D
Melody

Break

Bill Cheatem

Key of A

Salt Creek

Bill Monroe and Bradford Keith

Key of A
Melody

Break

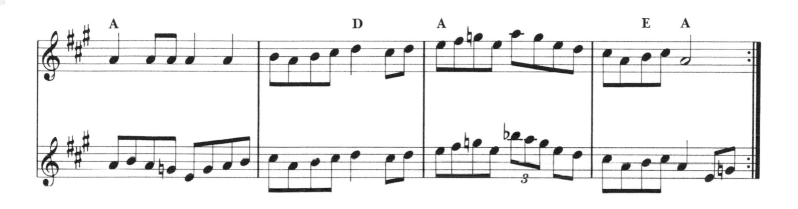

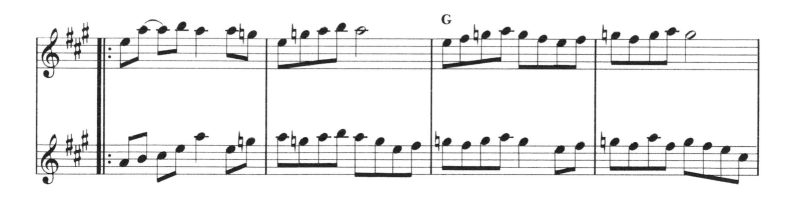

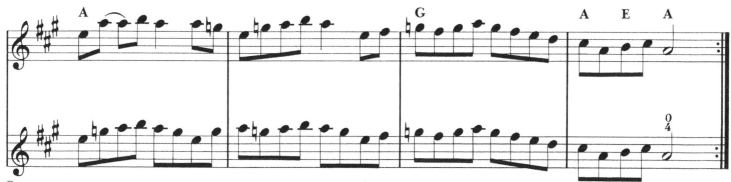

Sally Goodin

Playing Breaks

The single most important factor in taking a break is not the actual playing but rather the construction of the break, which is a mental process. No matter how well you play the fiddle, if you step up to the microphone with no idea of what you're going to play, it's not going to sound good.

There are basically two directions from which any improviser can approach his solo: melodically (horizontal) or harmonically (vertical). Although almost all improvisers use elements of both approaches, most players emphasize one over the other. In jazz, two tenor saxophone players are often cited as the leading exponents of the two schools—Lester Young, the melodic improviser, and Coleman Hawkins, the harmonic improviser. In bluegrass fiddling, one might point to Kenny Baker as an example of the melodic improviser and to Vassar Clements as the harmonic improviser.

The early bluegrass fiddlers, like Chubby Wise, were all solidly melodic in their approach. Chubby's breaks would usually consist of the melody with various ornamentations, like slides, neighboring notes and double stops. Harmonic improvisation is a relatively recent development in fiddling. In the past few years, as bluegrass absorbs more elements of jazz, a greater emphasis is being placed on instrumental virtuosity and hot licks; this is where the harmonic aspect comes into play. Rather than maintaining the shape of the melody in their breaks, modern players (like Vassar, Richard Greene or Rick Skaggs) have begun to play around the chord changes, craftily stringing licks together to move from one chord to the next.

The difference between these two approaches can best be illustrated by an example. A melodically-inclined fiddler might play the tune *Wabash Cannonball* something like this, altering the melody slightly and adding stops and slides:

etc.

But a modern "newgrass" fiddler might play it like this, by-passing the melody altogether and playing licks that go with the chords:

etc.

It's very important that the burgeoning improviser has a firm grasp of melodic playing before attempting to run the changes. When you feel comfortable playing the melody of a tune, you can then begin to add runs or licks as you feel they are appropriate.

When constructing a break, make sure that you save something special and interesting for the end of the solo; many beginning players make the mistake of using their best licks early on in the break and then have nothing to play at the end. Benny Martin was particularly brilliant at constructing breaks that had a surprise tag. Listen, for instance, to his break on the Flatt and Scruggs song, *Your Love Is Like a Flower,* available on Rounder Special Series 05. After a fairly straight melodic beginning, Benny plays this bizarre phrase in the final four bars:

Playing Backup

To my way of thinking, one of the most enjoyable things about bluegrass fiddling is getting to play backup. Here are some hints to help you avoid certain pitfalls that often present themselves in this area.

One of the most common mistakes a fiddler can make is to overplay while backing-up. It's important to remember that you're not playing a break underneath a vocal line but rather something that will complement and respond to what the singer is doing. There are spaces in songs, at the ending of phrases, where you can come up in both volume and intensity.

In the backup to the songs presented here, I've tried to include a lot of the standard devices a fiddler might use, such as double stops, runs and other fills. For the most part, I've chosen to omit (because of its repetitiveness) the most common backup technique, and that is the famous fiddle chunk. This effect (as if you couldn't tell from its name) is a rhythmic chunking sound that's produced by hitting the bow sharply against a double or triple stop that fits into the chord being played at the time. You can play chunks in a fairly straight rhythmic pattern as here:

or in a more complex pattern:

They can be interspersed with other backup devices in medium-tempo songs or used by themselves in very up-tempo tunes. Keep in mind that smaller intervals (such as thirds) generally sound better than more open intervals (such as sixths). Also, if you play chunks right near the frog, you'll find you get a crisper, more biting attack than anywhere else on the bow.

A left-hand technique that's very effective in medium tempo and slow songs is moving double stops. An example of this technique is the first line of backup to *Live and Let Live*.

The Tunes

All the tunes in the next part of the book, with the exception of *John Hardy*, are vocals. Bluegrass is primarily a vocal music, where the instruments are used to backup the singing and take breaks between verses. (This is not to denigrate the instruments but merely to put the vocals where they belong.)

As in most of this book, the music is presented in a format similar to piano music, with two staves barred together. On the top staff of every system is the melody of the tune; on the bottom staff is a break or some backup licks. There are five songs presented with backup: *Salty Dog, Dark Hollow, Little Maggie, All the Good Times* and *Will the Circle Be Unbroken.* In these cases, the music with melody and backup appears first, followed immediately by the arrangement with melody and a break. Although not too widely divergent in terms of difficulty, the breaks do present different fiddling techniques, some of which I'd like to point out.

Salty Dog is high on the "Ten Most-Played Songs in Bluegrass" list. Both the break and the backup are taken, almost note-for-note, from Herb Hooven's playing on the album *Living on the Mountain* (Prestige-Folklore 14002). There is a moderate use of double stops and slides here, as well as some classic eight-note runs. The break to *Dark Hollow* is very similar to what Randall Collins plays on the country album *Shadows of Time*—sweet and lyrical, with some jazzy syncopations towards the end. (Also, not the absence of double stops in this one.)

All the Good Times is an up-tempo tune in waltz time, which is uncommon in bluegrass. The break is fairly melodic, as are those to *Little Maggie* and *Nine Pound Hammer. John Hardy* (the only instrumental in this section) is good practice for playing in second position up until the D chord at the end, at which point you should shift back to first position.

Pretty Polly is a song of the type often done by Ralph Stanley—lonesome mountain music. Being a modal tune, the tonality should remain fairly ambiguous; if you're playing with chordal instruments, have the guitar player play an A minor chord, with no emphasis on the third. (Remember, you don't want to sound like the Kingston Trio on this type of number.) The break captures some of the flavor of Curly Ray Cline's fiddling.

Will the Circle Be Unbroken and *Sitting on Top of the World* have breaks that are a bit more challenging than that previous ones in this section. Notice that they both end with this classic lick:

The backup to *Circle* contains some Vassar Clements-style licks, particularly the run in measure four.

In *Live and Let Live,* both backup and break are Kenny Baker-ish, especially measures 14–16 in the backup and measures 5 through 8 in the break. Remember, this is in the key of B, with five sharps; count 'em, five!

Salty Dog

Key of G

Melody

G   E   A

Let me be your sal - ty dog or I won't be your man at all,

Backup

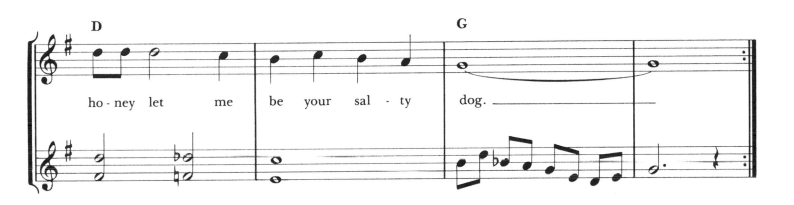

D   G

ho - ney let   me   be your sal - ty   dog._____

Key of G

Melody

G   E   A

Let me be your sal - ty dog or I won't be your man at all,

Break

D   G

ho - ney let   me   be your sal - ty   dog._____

Dark Hollow

I'd ra-ther be ____ in some ____ dark hol-low ____

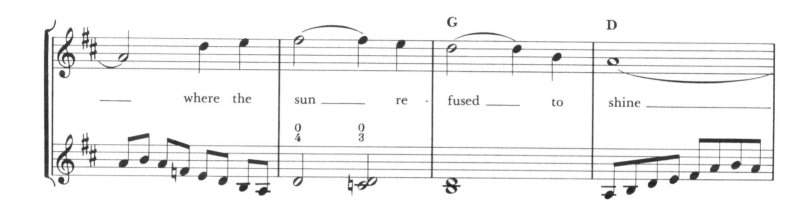

____ where the sun ____ re-fused ____ to shine ____

____ than to be at home a-lone, know-in' that you're

gone ____ would cause me to lose ____ my mind. ____

Dark Hollow

Key of D

Melody

Break

I'd ra - ther be ____ in some ____ dark hol - low ____

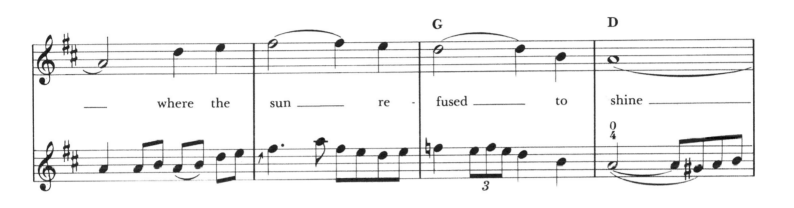

____ where the sun ____ re - fused ____ to shine ____

____ than to be at home a - lone, know - in' that you're

gone ____ would cause me to lose ____ my mind. ____

Little Maggie

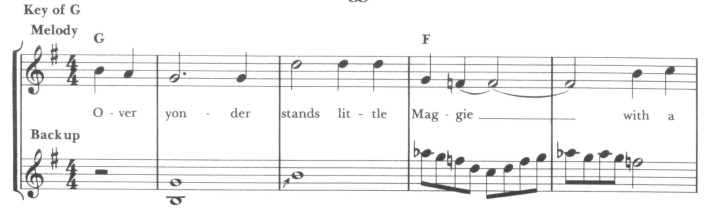

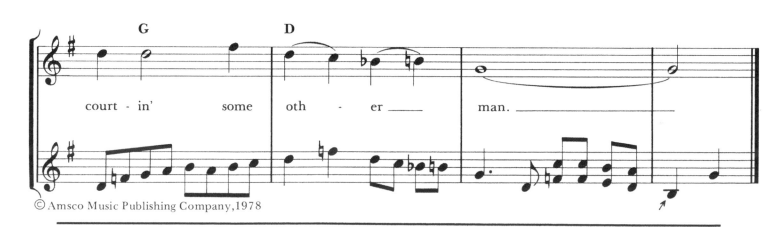

Little Maggie

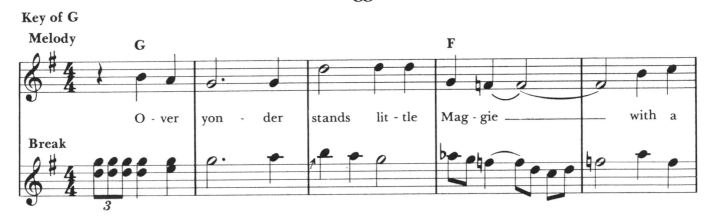

O - ver yon - der stands lit - tle Mag - gie ——— with a

dram glass in ——— her ——— hand. ——————— she's ———

drin - kin' a - way her trou - bles ——————— by

court - in' some oth - er ——— man. ———————

All the Good Times Are Past and Gone

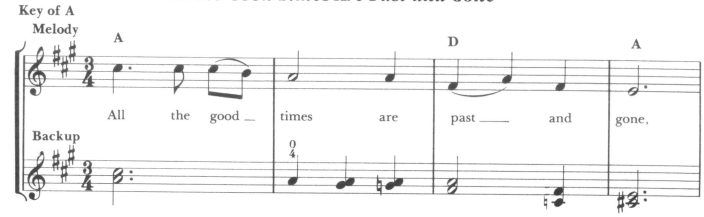

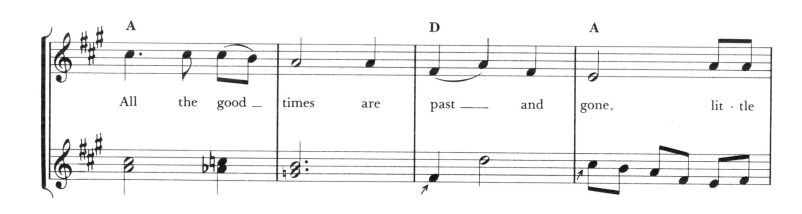

All the Good Times Are Past and Gone

Key of A
Melody

All the good times are past and gone,

Break

All the good times are o'er.

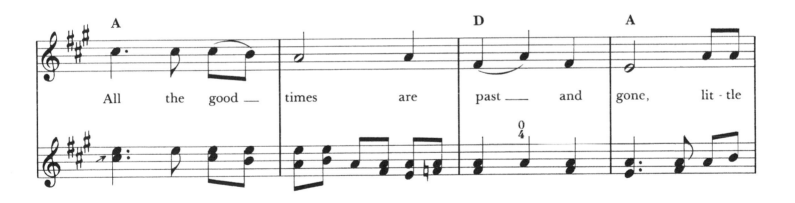

All the good times are past and gone, lit - tle

dar - lin' don't you weep no more.

Nine Pound Hammer

John Hardy

Key of G
Melody

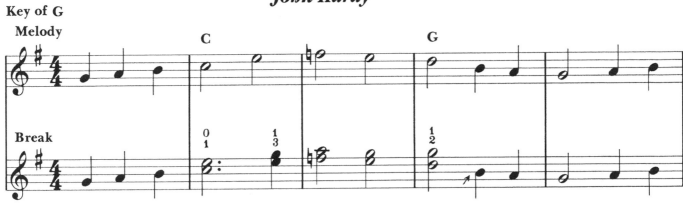

Break

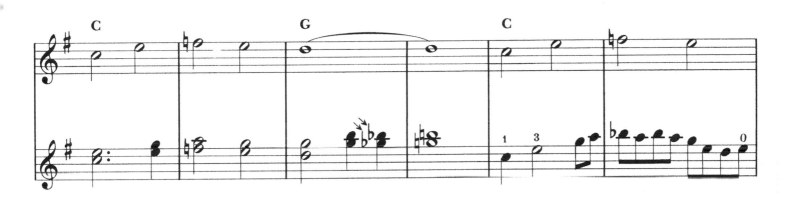

Pretty Polly

Key of A modal

Melody

Oh,   Pol - ly,   pretty   Pol - ly,   come   go   a - long with   me.

Break

Pol - ly,   pretty   Pol - ly,   come   go   a - long with   me,   be-

fore   we   get   mar - ried, some   plea - sure   to   see.

Sitting on Top of the World

Key of A
Melody

It was in the spring _____ one sun-ny day, _____ my good gal

left ___ me, _____ she went a-way. _____ But now she's

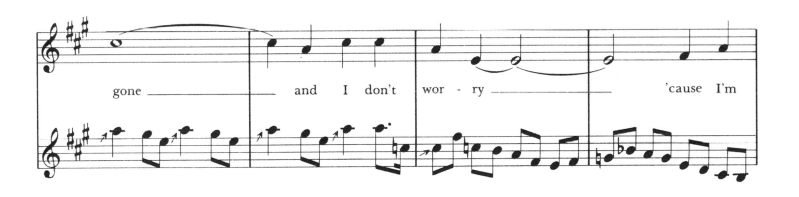

gone _____ and I don't wor-ry _____ 'cause I'm

sit-tin' on top of the world. _____

Will the Circle Be Unbroken

Key of D

Will the cir - cle be un - bro - ken by and

by, Lord, by and by. _____ There's a bet - ter home a-

wait - in' in the sky, Lord, in the sky. _____

Will the Circle Be Unbroken

Will the cir - cle be un - bro - ken. By and

by, Lord, by and by. _____ There's a bett - er home a-

wait - in' in the sky, Lord, in the sky. _____

Live and Let Live

Key of B

Wiley Walker and Gene Sullivan

Live____ and let live, don't____ break my heart; don't

leave me here to cry.____ I

ne - ver could live if____ we should part;

tell me____ you don't mean____ good - bye.____

Key of B
Melody

Live and Let Live

Wiley Walker and Gene Sullivan

Live___ and let live, do - n't break my heart; don't

leave me here to cry.___ I

ne - ver could live if ___ we should part;

tell me ___ you don't mean _____ good - bye. _____

Roll in My Sweet Baby's Arms

Key of A
Melody

Break

I ain't gon - na work on the rail - road, _____

_____ ain't gon - na work on the farm. _____

_____ I'll just lay a - round _____ my shack 'til the mail train gets

back, and roll in my sweet ba - by's arms. _____

The Fiddle

The most common question that a fiddler is liable to be asked is "What's the difference between a violin and a fiddle?" And of course the weary fiddler should respond politely, "no difference." The word "fiddle" is merely a nickname for the violin that applies whenever the instrument is used to play folk, country, or popular music.

There are a few differences, however, concerning the set-up of the instrument, depending on which kind of music you want to play. Where a classical violinist would use steel-wound gut strings, the bluegrass fiddler would use regular steel strings. There are basically three reasons why this is so: (1) to facilitate the use of fine tuners on the tailpiece, (2) to achieve the volume necessary for the fiddle to be heard in a band context, and (3) to permit the fiddler to play hard for long periods of time without the strings wearing down.

In addition to the use of the steel strings, some fiddlers have their bridges cut flatter than what is standard for a violin. Supposedly, this makes it easier to play double stops, but I don't think it's really necessary. For whatever facility you gain in playing double stops, you lose that much in playing single string lines.

Some people labor under the mistaken impression that to play bluegrass fiddle, one's violin must be covered with rosin from the bow. Accumulated rosin dust can only do harm to your instrument, and it's advisable to clean your fiddle periodically. Running a soft cloth or rag underneath the bridge and fingerboard should do the trick.

There are number of qualities that one should look for in a fiddle. For playing bluegrass, your instrument should be good and loud, so it can be heard when you play with other musicians. The tone should be fairly sweet, not raspy or metallic; also, avoid fiddles with a painfully piercing upper register.

Each instrument is different from the next and you should choose one that suits your musical temperament.

More Tunes

Two vocal numbers, four rare fiddle tunes and one double fiddle tune make up the final section of music in this book.

High Dad in the Morning is a rare fiddle tune that Kenny Baker plays on the record *Portrait of a Bluegrass Fiddler,* Country 719. Not only does it have three parts instead of the traditional two, but there are an extra two beats in the second part.

Footprints in the Snow is a bluegrass gem made popular by Bill Monroe. The break closely resembles Charlie Cline's version, with elements of the Chubby Wise rendition added for good measure. Although the break is presented for both verse and chorus, you will usually only have to solo on the verse (By the way, if anyone understands the hidden meaning of these lyrics, I wish they'd write me a letter.)

John Henry is a great traditional tune, but the break given here is the most modern in the book. It's basically a compendium of "newgrass" licks á la Ricky Skaggs.

Cattle in the Corn is a beautiful modal tune, the first part of which is in A major and the second part in A minor. This is the Joe Green version of the tune, as available on County 722

June Apple is a popular modal fiddle tune that lends itself well to double fiddles. Playing twin with another fiddler is at once very demanding and very rewarding. If you take the time to work out the same bowings and phrasing, twin fiddling can be one of the most enjoyable musical experiences you'll ever have.

Blue Eagle (not to be confused with *Grey Eagle*) is a Texas fiddle tune that I feel could fit well into the repertoire of a bluegrass band. This is a transcription of the version played by the Ophelia Swing Band on their Biscuit City recording, BC 1313.

The final tune in this book, *Crazy Creek,* has a number of unusual characteristics. In the A part, the fiddle consistently plays a C$\sharp$ note against an A minor chord in the other instruments; this creates a certain kind of tension. In addition, the bridge modulates to the key of F major. (The tune as an AABA structure.) A fine recording of this tune can be heard on Bryon Berline's *Pickin' and Fiddlin'* album with the Dillards.

High Dad in the Morning

Key of Em

Footprints in the Snow

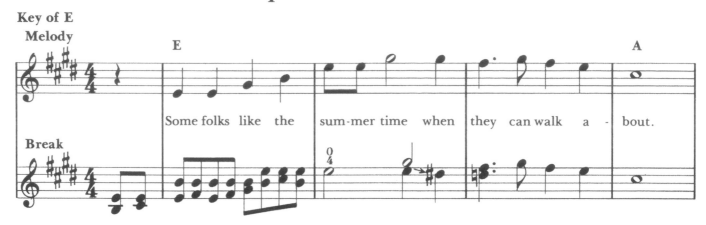

Some folks like the sum-mer time when they can walk a - bout.

Stroll - ing through the mea - dow green it's plea - sant there's no doubt.

But give me the win - ter time when the snow was on the ground, for I

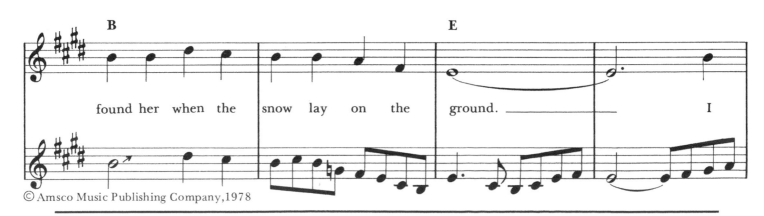

found her when the snow lay on the ground. _____ I

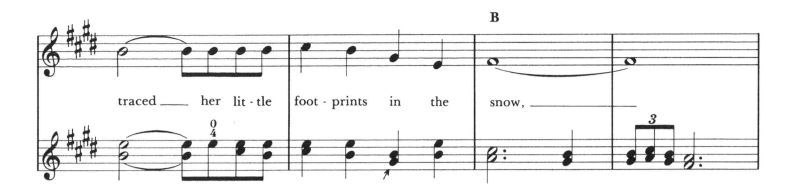

traced ____ her lit - tle foot - prints in the snow, ____

found ____ her lit - tle foot - prints in the snow. Lord, ____

bless that hap - py day ____ when Nel - lie lost her way, for I

found her when the snow was on the ground. ____

John Henry

Key of G

John Hen-ry was a lit - tle ba - by boy, you could hold him in the

palm of your hand. _____ His pa - pa cried out this

2 3 4 0 0

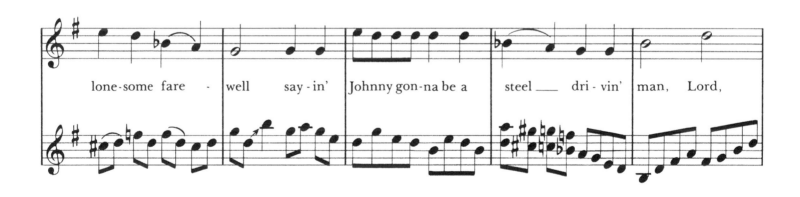

lone-some fare - well say - in' Johnny gon-na be a steel ___ dri - vin' man, Lord,

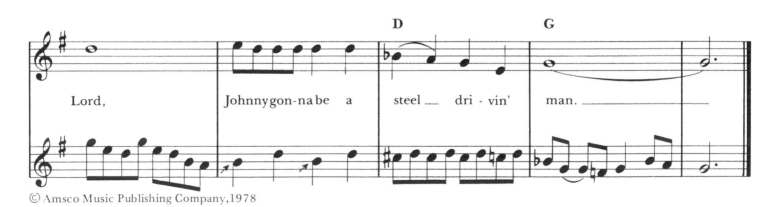

Lord, Johnny gon-na be a steel ___ dri - vin' man. _____

Cattle in the Corn

Key of A
Melody

Break

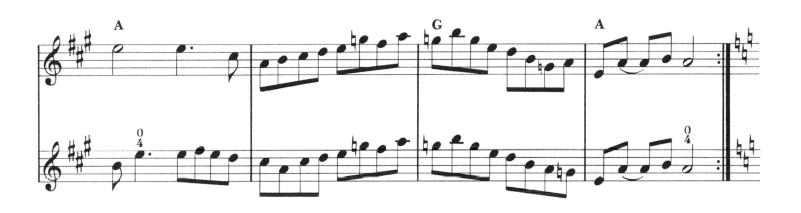

June Apple

Key of A modal (no G♯)
1st fiddle

2nd fiddle

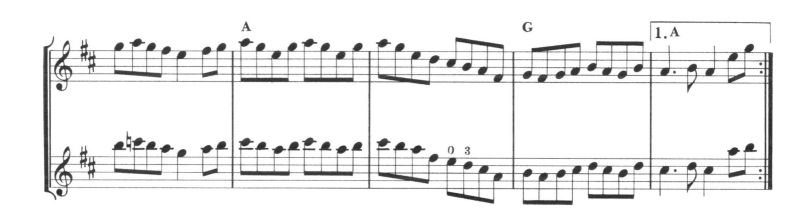

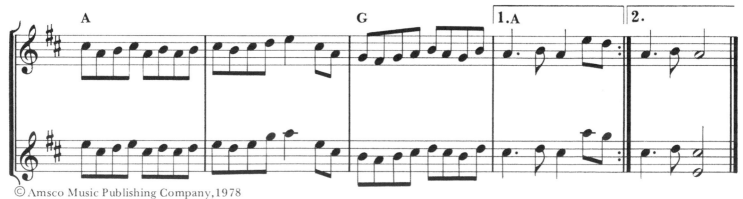

© Amsco Music Publishing Company, 1978

Blue Eagle

Key of D

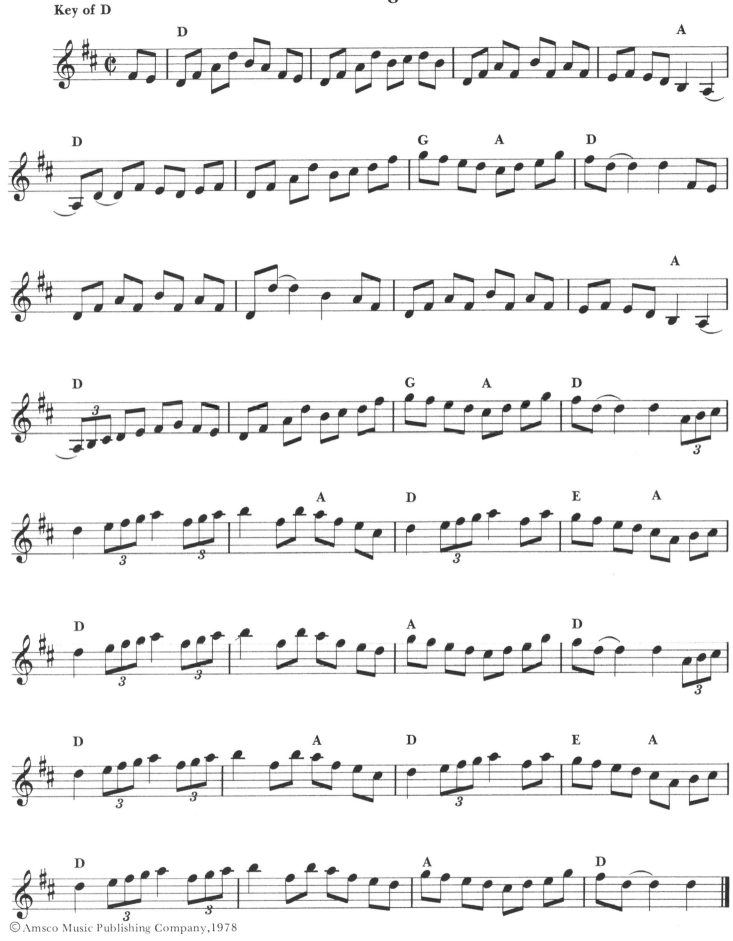

Crazy Creek

Key of Am
Melody

Break

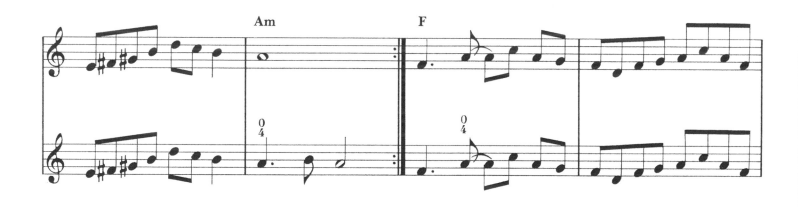

Discography

There are a lot of good bluegrass fiddle CDs around. Any recording of the fiddlers mentioned in this book is good to have. Here are some that I think are particularly fine.

Kenny Baker
Master Fiddle (County 2705)
Plays Bill Monroe (County 2708)

Vassar Clements
The Bluegrass Sessions (Flying Fish 38)

Stuart Duncan
Stuart Duncan (Rounder 263)

Bill Monroe
Bill Monroe 1950-58 (Bear Family BCD-15423)
Bill Monroe 1959-69 (Bear Family BCD-11529-4)

All of the above CDs, with the exception of Bill Monroe, were put out under the fiddler's own name. Most of the great bluegrass fiddling recordings, however, were recorded under the names of the artists other than the fiddlers themselves. Here are some of those CDs, with the name of the fiddler in bold italics.

Doc & Merle Watson with ***Byron Berline***
Red Rocking Chair (Flying Fish 252)

Flatt & Scruggs with ***Benny Martin*** and others
Don't Get Above Your Raisin' (Rounder CD-SS-08)

Various Artists with ***Herb Hooven***
Rounder Bluegrass, Vol. 1 (Rounder CD-11511)

Jim & Jesse with ***Jim Buchanan*** and others
The Jim & Jesse Story: 24 Greatest (CMH 9022)

Nitty Gritty Dirt Band with ***Vassar Clements***
Will the Circle Be Unbroken, Vol. 2 (MCA 12500)

Earl Scruggs Revue with ***Vassar Clements***
Artists Choice: The Best Tracks (1970-1980) (Edsel 552)

The Kentucky Colonels with ***Scotty Stoneman***
Kentucky Colonels (Beat Goes On 357)